I Like to Visit

The Shopping Mall

Jacqueline Laks Gorman

Reading consultant: Susan Nations, M.Ed.,
author/literacy coach/consultant

Please visit our web site at: www.earlyliteracy.cc
For a free color catalog describing Weekly Reader® Early Learning Library's list of high-quality books, call 1-877-445-5824 (USA) or 1-800-387-3178 (Canada). Weekly Reader® Early Learning Library's fax: (414) 336-0164.

Library of Congress Cataloging-in-Publication Data

Gorman, Jacqueline Laks, 1955–
   The shopping mall / Jacqueline Laks Gorman.
      p. cm. — (I like to visit)
   Includes bibliographical references and index.
   ISBN 0-8368-4455-6 (lib. bdg.)
   ISBN 0-8368-4462-9 (softcover)
   1. Shopping malls—Juvenile literature. I. Title. II. Series.
   HF5430.G665   2005
   381'.11—dc22   2004057165

This edition first published in 2005 by
Weekly Reader® Early Learning Library
330 West Olive Street, Suite 100
Milwaukee, WI 53212 USA

Art direction: Tammy West
Editor: JoAnn Early Macken
Cover design and page layout: Kami Koenig
Picture research: Diane Laska-Swanke

Picture credits: Cover, pp. 5, 7, 9, 11, 13, 15, 17, 19, 21 Gregg Andersen

Printed in the United States of America

1 2 3 4 5 6 7 8 9 09 08 07 06 05

Note to Educators and Parents

Reading is such an exciting adventure for young children! They are beginning to integrate their oral language skills with written language. To encourage children along the path to early literacy, books must be colorful, engaging, and interesting; they should invite the young reader to explore both the print and the pictures.

I Like to Visit is a new series designed to help children read about familiar and exciting places. Each book explores a different place that kids like to visit and describes what a visitor can see and do there.

Each book is specially designed to support the young reader in the reading process. The familiar topics are appealing to young children and invite them to read — and re-read — again and again. The full-color photographs and enhanced text further support the student during the reading process.

In addition to serving as wonderful picture books in schools, libraries, homes, and other places where children learn to love reading, these books are specifically intended to be read within an instructional guided reading group. This small group setting allows beginning readers to work with a fluent adult model as they make meaning from the text. After children develop fluency with the text and content, the book can be read independently. Children and adults alike will find these books supportive, engaging, and fun!

— Susan Nations, M.Ed., author, literacy coach, and consultant in literacy development

I like to visit the shopping mall. I like to visit the stores. I like to go shopping with my family.

Here is a map of
the mall. The map
is near the door.
I can look at the
map. I can find the
stores on the map.

YOU ARE ON LEVEL 1

I like to ride on the escalator. The stairs move up and down. I can ride upstairs and ride back down.

The mall is big.
I can see many
stores. I always
stay with my family.

This store sells art supplies. I like to look at the paints.

This store sells toys.
I like to play with
the stuffed animals.

This store sells books. I like to go in and read them.

This store sells clothes. I will try on a hat.

Now I am hungry.
I like to eat in the
food court. I like to
eat pizza. What do
you like to eat?

Glossary

escalator — a set of stairs that keeps moving up or down

map — a drawing of an area that shows where things are found

shopping mall — a group of stores. Some shopping malls are all inside one building. Others are groups of buildings.

For More Information

Books

The Awful Aardvarks Shop for School. Reeve Lindbergh (Viking)

Behind the Scenes at the Shopping Mall. Marilyn Miller (Raintree/Steck-Vaughn)

I'm Safe! At the Mall. I'm Safe! (series). Wendy Gordon (BackYard Books)

Malls: The Sound of M. Cynthia Klingel and Peg Ballard (Child's World)

Web Sites

Brain Pop
www.brainpop.com/math/problemsolving/com paringprices/index.weml?&tried_cookie=true
Comparing Prices

Index

art supplies 12

books 16

clothes 18

eating 20

escalators 8

food 20

hats 18

maps 6

paints 12

stuffed animals 14

toys 14

pizza 20

About the Author

Jacqueline Laks Gorman is a writer and editor. She grew up in New York City and began her career working on encyclopedias and other reference books. Since then, she has worked on many different kinds of books and written several children's books. She lives with her husband, David, and children, Colin and Caitlin, in DeKalb, Illinois. They all like to visit many kinds of places.